T0066232

THE BAND METHOD THAT TEACHES MUSIC READING

# RHYTHM

# MASTER

**Supplemental Material**

By

J.R. McEntyre
Coordinator of Music, Retired
Odessa Public Schools
Odessa, Texas

And

Harry H. Haines
Music Department Chairman
West Texas State University
Canyon, Texas

L. Chris Arrowood, Percussion Editor

# Preliminary Lesson
## The Most Important Lesson!

Some aspects of learning to play a band instrument are best learned without an instruction book. This is especially true of the very first stages such as 1) putting the instrument together, 2) learning correct posture and position, and 3) producing the sound. Also, an understanding of a few basic music symbols will be a great help in beginning to read a method book. The authors believe that best results will be achieved if the teacher approaches this lesson using a Suzuki-like presentation. The basis should be rote teaching using much imitation and repetition.

The **Conductor's Guide** contains specific information about each instrument and suggestions from a master teacher for introducing the proper hand position.

How long should you spend on a **Preliminary Lesson**? Teaching situations vary but most successful beginning band classes we know get better results when they spend four or five hours on this material. At a minimum, hand positions and proper method of motion should be established to a point where students are able to consistently produce the stroke for their first note in **LESSON 1**.

**1** Start with one stick only. Your teacher will show you how to hold the stick. A proper hand position is a must in order to produce a good stroke.

**2** Work on correct posture. Pay careful attention to your teacher's instructions. Good posture is an acquired habit and the time to start is the first day.

**3** Put the instrument together properly and learn to set its height correctly. Practice this many times until you can do it well. Instruments may look strong but they are really quite delicate and are easily damaged. Each student must learn how to care for his/her instrument and there will never be a better time than now.

**4** Produce a characteristic stroke and sound. To do this requires much repetition. Every person learns to play an instrument by the "trial and error" method. One of the essential aspects of success is to "try" enough times to give the method a chance for learning to occur. Repetition, correct instruction, and constant, intelligent analysis are the three primary aspects of learning to play an instrument. The most important of these is (you guessed it) _repetition_! You must go over and over your basic stroke and sound always trying to make them better.

**5** Practice alternating. Start the stroke with one hand and then strike with the other. Learning the basics of percussion is a matter of coordinating single hand <u>and</u> alternating strokes. This should be a major goal of this **Preliminary Lesson**.

**6** Finally, every student must learn a few basic music symbols before he/she can begin to read music. **LESSON 1** will be much easier if you know the musical terms below. Throughout this book, the red, numbered flags refer to the **Index of Musical Terms** found on the back cover.

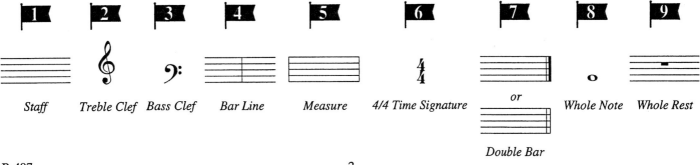

| Staff | Treble Clef | Bass Clef | Bar Line | Measure | 4/4 Time Signature | Double Bar | Whole Note | Whole Rest |

# Snare Drum
### How to Hold the Sticks

There are two methods that are generally accepted by most percussion teachers: the traditional grip and the matched grip. Both systems are widely used and successful. The method selected is left to the discretion of the individual teachers. Both are explained here:

## Matched Grip

The snare drum sticks should be held as naturally as possible. Grasp the stick firmly between the thumb and the middle joint of the index finger, approximately one inch behind the balance point of the stick (towards the end). Wrap the remaining fingers loosely around the stick, making sure the palm of your hand is parallel to the floor. Finger action, combined with wrist and arm movements provide all the necessary control.

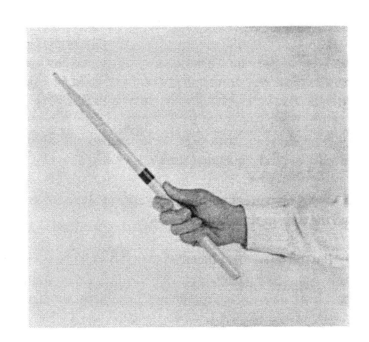

## Traditional Grip

For the traditional grip, the right hand is the same as in the matched grip system. The left hand, however, is considerably different. With your thumb up, palm perpendicular to the floor, and elbow relaxed by your side, place the back end of the stick snugly between your ring and third fingers. Allow the index finger to wrap loosely around the stick. Keep the "pinky" finger pulled back beneath the ring finger to add support and prevent the hand from collapsing into a fist. Always keep your hands and wrists relaxed. This style of grip is excellent for developing the strength and dexterity needed for four-mallet skills (Musser grip).

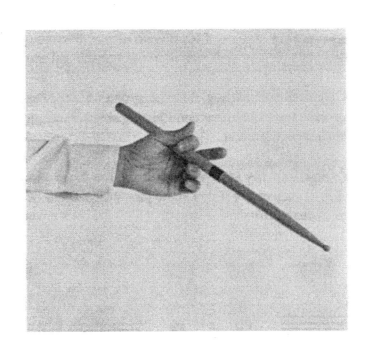

# Snare Drum
## Proper Playing Position

### Adjusting the Snare or Pad

To find the proper height for the drum, drop the arms to your sides, then raise them to a relaxed and comfortable position. There should be a slight downward angle from the elbows, through the hands, to the tips of the sticks. Adjust the pad or drum height so that the drum head is one inch below the tips of the sticks, when held as described above. Never rest the tips of the sticks on the drum. Always remember to adjust the height of the drum to the player; the player should not have to adjust to the height of the drum.

### Position of the Sticks

Play so that the tips of the sticks strike in the center of the drum or pad and the sticks are at a slightly greater than ninety-degree angle to each other.

# Bells
## How to Hold the Sticks/Proper Playing Position

Only the *matched grip* is used when playing the mallet instruments (see p. 4). The grip is the same, but the placement on the stick is different. When playing mallet instruments, hold the mallet or stick as close to the end as possible.

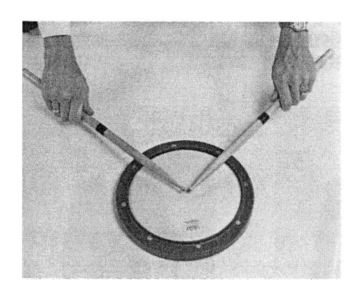

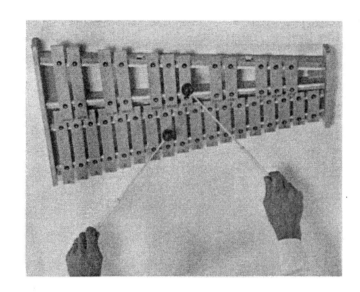

## Playing Position and Height Adjustment

Most concert mallet instruments (orchestra bells, xylophone, vibraphone, or marimba) cannot be adjusted by height. Luckily, most bell kits can. Adjusting the height of the bell kit is the same as adjusting the height of the snare drum or pad, as previously explained (see p. 5). Stand back from the mallet instrument, so you can see the instrument, the music, and the conductor at the same time. Always strike the center of the bar for the best sound. Finally, always try to center your body in the current playing area of the mallet instrument.

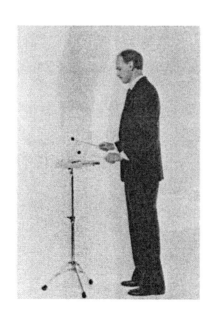

# Bells
## Four-Mallet Grip

### How to Play with Two Sticks in Each Hand

Playing with four mallets (two in each hand) allows the percussionist to increase the complexity of the harmonic and melodic lines, including complete chordal accompaniments. It also develops independence between the hands. The grip that is demonstrated below is the Musser grip, developed by the famous marimbist Omar Musser.

The first (lower) mallet is held between the ring and middle fingers so that the ring and little fingers are gripping the mallet. The end of the mallet is placed at the base of the little finger. The second (upper) mallet is held between the tip of the thumb and the first joint of the index finger, with the end of the mallet resting in the middle of the palm. The tip of the middle finger rests near the end of the second mallet to hold it in place.

The distance between the two mallets in one hand is controlled by the thumb and index finger holding the upper mallet; extend for wider intervals, and contract for smaller intervals. The position of the lower mallet does not change.

To play the two mallets in one hand at the same time, use an up and down motion, keeping the wrist straight and bending at the elbow. To play each mallet independently, use a rotating motion at the wrist, as used in the left hand of the traditional grip.

Before introducing the four-mallet grip, the student should have completely mastered the skills needed for two-mallet playing through **Lesson 13**. When the teacher determines that the student is ready for four-mallet playing, the student should return to **Lesson 1** and play through the book again, using the Musser grip.

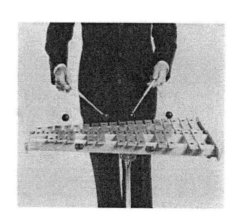

**Rudiment:** **Single Stroke**

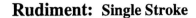

R     L     R     L

*R = right hand; L = left hand*

**1** **The First Note**   *Repeat many times.*

| | These "flag" symbols indicate something new. The numbers refer to the **Index of Musical Terms** on the back cover. |
|---|---|

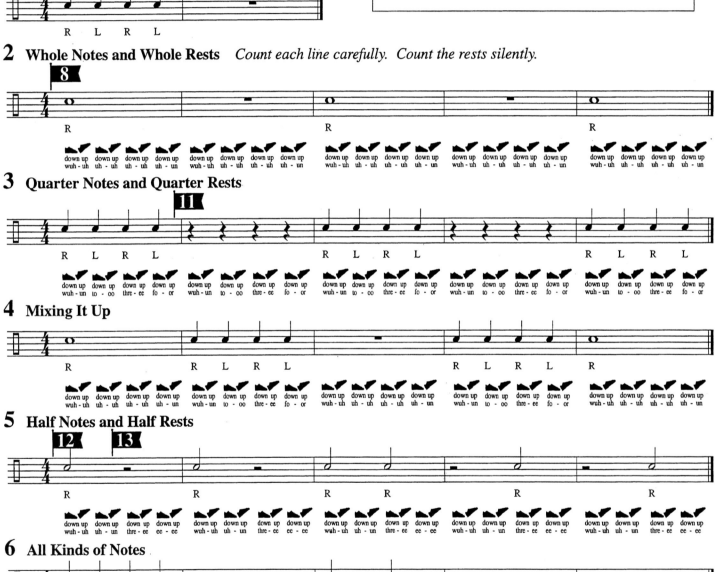

**2** **Whole Notes and Whole Rests**   *Count each line carefully.  Count the rests silently.*

**3** **Quarter Notes and Quarter Rests**

**4** **Mixing It Up**

**5** **Half Notes and Half Rests**

**6** **All Kinds of Notes**

**7** **All Kinds of Rests**   *Write the counting on the lines below the staff.*

# LESSON 1
## The First Note

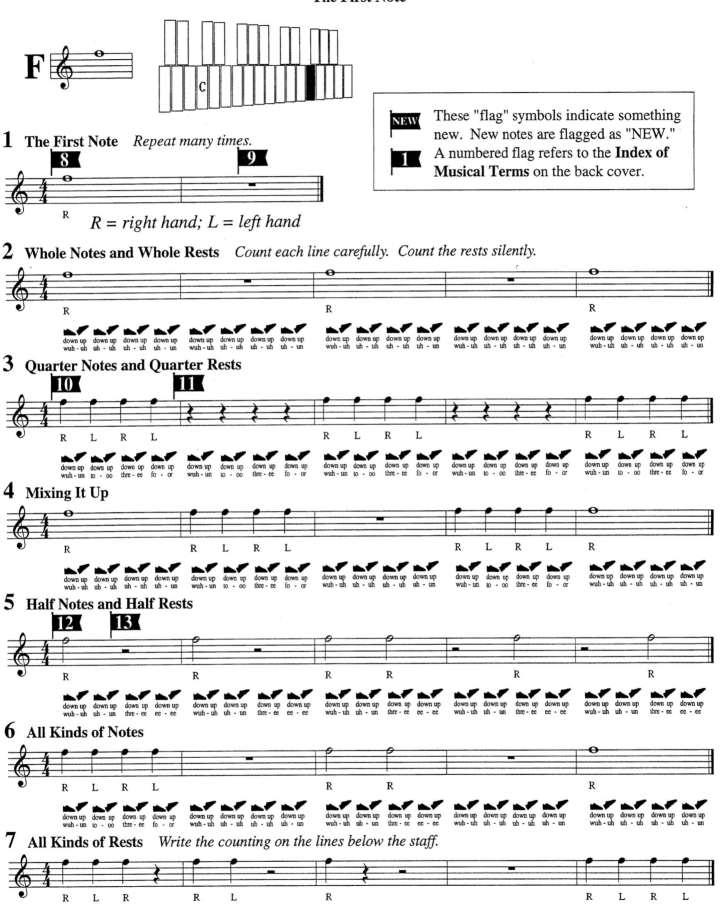

**F**

**1 The First Note** *Repeat many times.*

R = right hand; L = left hand

**NEW** These "flag" symbols indicate something new. New notes are flagged as "NEW."

**1** A numbered flag refers to the **Index of Musical Terms** on the back cover.

**2 Whole Notes and Whole Rests** *Count each line carefully. Count the rests silently.*

**3 Quarter Notes and Quarter Rests**

**4 Mixing It Up**

**5 Half Notes and Half Rests**

**6 All Kinds of Notes**

**7 All Kinds of Rests** *Write the counting on the lines below the staff.*

# LESSON 2
## The Second Note

**Rudiment:** **Diddle** *Two consecutive beats by the same hand.*

*Tap your foot, count, and play every line.*

*SUGGESTION: Start every class using Warm-up #1 on the inside of the front cover.*

# LESSON 2
## The Second Note

**8  The Second Note**  *Repeat many times.*

**9  Practice the New Note**

*Tap your foot, count, and play every line.*

**10  Two-Note Song**  *Write the counting on the lines below the staff.*

**11  First Duet**

**12  Duet Part**

**13  Quarter Notes and Quarter Rests**

**14  All Kinds of Notes**

**15  Who Will Play in the Rest?**

*SUGGESTION: Start every class using Warm-up #1 on the inside of the front cover.*

# LESSON 3
## Three Notes

**Rudiment:** **Multiple Bounce**  *The multiple bounce, or "buzz," roll is produced by letting the stick bounce as many times as possible per note length.*

R   L   R   L

**16  The Third Note**  *Repeat many times.*

*Good players can read music.  Remember to tap your foot, count, and play every line.*

R   L   R   L

**17  Three-Note Exercise**

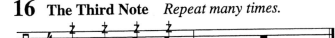

R   L       R   L       R   L       R   L   R   L

| down up | down up | down up | down up | down up | down up | down up | down up | down up | down up | down up | down up | down up | down up | down up | down up |
| wuh-un | to-oo | thre-ee | ee-ee | wuh-un | to-oo | thre-ee | ee-ee | wuh-un | to-oo | thre-ee | ee-ee | wuh-un | to-oo | thre-ee | fo-or |

**18  Echo Song**

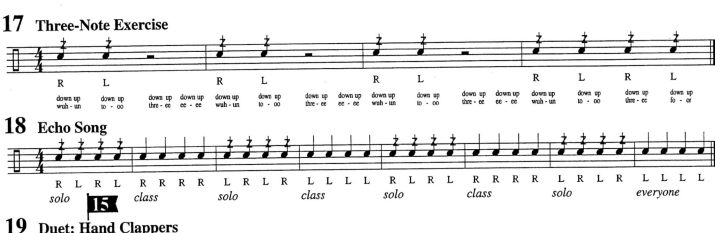

R L R L   R R R R   L R L R   L L L L   R L R L   R R R R   L R L R   L L L L

*solo*  **15**  *class*       *solo*       *class*       *solo*       *class*       *solo*       *everyone*

**19  Duet: Hand Clappers**

R L R L       R L R       R L       R       L

**20  Duet: Finger Snappers**

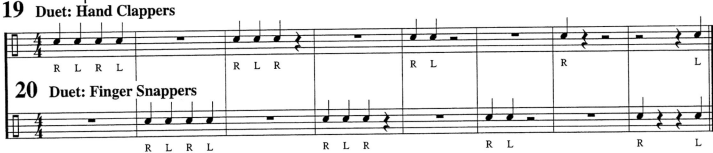

R L R L       R L R       R L       R       L

**21  All Kinds of Notes**

R L R L   R L R L   R R L L   R L R L   R L R       R L R       R L R       R L R L

**22  Who Will Play in the Rest (Again)?**

R L R L       L R L   R L R L       L R L   R L R L       L R L   R L R L       L R L

**23  Our First Song**

R R L L   R L R L   R L R L   R L R L   R R L L   R L R L   R R L L   R L R L

B-497

12

# LESSON 3
## Three Notes

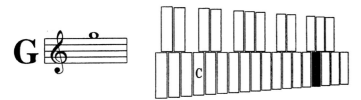

G

**16** **The Third Note**  *Repeat many times.*

NEW

R
L

*Good players can read music. Remember to tap your foot, count, and play every line.*

**17** **Three-Note Exercise**

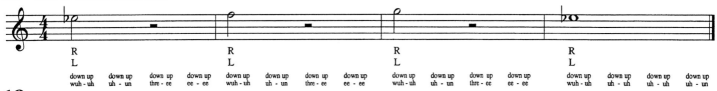

R       R       R       R
L       L       L       L

down up  down up  down up  down up  down up  down up  down up  down up  down up  down up  down up  down up  down up  down up  down up  down up
wuh-uh   uh-un    thre-ee  ee-ee    wuh-uh   uh-un    thre-ee  ee-ee    wuh-uh   uh-un    thre-ee  ee-ee    wuh-uh   uh-uh    uh-uh    uh-un

**18** **Echo Song**

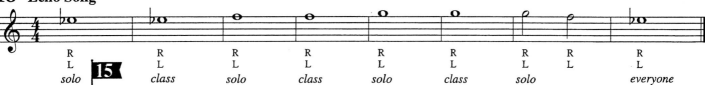

R       R       R       R       R       R       R       R       R
L       L       L       L       L       L       L       L       L

solo  **15**  class   solo    class   solo    class   solo              everyone

**19** **Duet: Hand Clappers**

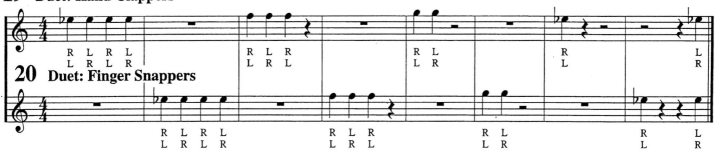

R L R L         R L R           R L             R                     L
L R L R         L R L           L R             L                     R

**20** **Duet: Finger Snappers**

R L R L         R L R           R L             R                     L
L R L R         L R L           L R             L                     R

**21** **All Kinds of Notes**

R L R L    R    R L R L    R R    R L R    R L R    R L R    R
L R L R    L    L R L R    L L    L R L    L R L    L R L    L

**22** **Who Will Play in the Rest (Again)?**

R         L R L    R R    L R L    R R    L R L    R R    L R
L         R L R    L L    R L R    L L    R L R    L L    R L

**23** **Our First Song**

R R L L    R L R    R L R    R L R    R R L L    R L R    R R L L    R
L L R R    L R L    L R L    L R L    L L R R    L R L    L L R R    L

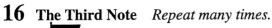

# LESSON 4
## The Eighth Note Lesson

*Always carry your instrument
case with the lid toward you.*

**Rudiment:** Eighth Note Diddles

R  R  L  L  R  R  L  L

**24** **Introducing Eighth Notes**

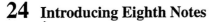

R  R  L  L  R  R  L  L  R  L  R  L  R  R  L  L  R  R  L  L  R  L  R  L

down up down up down up down up  down up down up down up down up  down up down up down up down up  down up down up down up down up

**25** **Eighth Notes and Quarter Notes**  *Write the counting on the lines below the staff.*

R  R  L  R  L  R  R  L  R  L  R  R  L  R  L  R  L  R  L

**26** **Sneaky Second Count**

R  L  L  R  L  R  L  L  R  L  R  L  L  R  L  R  L  R  L

**27** **Tricky Third Count**

R  L  R  R  L  R  L  R  R  L  R  L  R  R  L  R  L  R  L

**28** **Freaky Fourth Count**

R  L  R  L  L  R  L  R  L  L  R  L  R  L  L  R  L  R  L

**29** **All Mixed Up**

*SPECIAL ASSIGNMENT:  Before going to line 29, try to count and play the first measures of 25, 26, 27, and 28 straight down the page. Then do the second measures, then the third, etc. This is a great exercise in rhythm!*

R  R  L  R  L  R  L  L  R  L  R  L  R  R  L  R  L

**30** **Hot Cross Buns**

R  L  R  R  L  R  R  R  L  L  R  R  L  L  R  L  R

**31** **Merrily We Speed Along** *Use both stickings; #2 alternating throughout.*

1. R  R  R  L  L  R  R  L  R  R  L  R  R  L  R  R  L  L  R  R  L  L  R  R  L  L  R  L
2. R  L  R  L  R  L  R  L  R  L  R  L  R  L  R  L  R  L  R  L  R  L  R  L  R  L  R  L

# LESSON 4
## The Eighth Note Lesson

*Always carry your instrument case with the lid toward you.*

**24** **Introducing Eighth Notes**

R R L L R R L L    R        R R L L R R L L    R

down up down up down up down up    down up down up down up down up    down up down up down up down up    down up down up down up down up

**25** **Eighth Notes and Quarter Notes**   *Write the counting on the lines below the staff.*

R R L R L   R R L R L   R R L R L   R

**26** **Sneaky Second Count**

R L L R L   R L L R L   R L L R L   R

**27** **Tricky Third Count**

R L R R L   R L R R L   R L R R L   R

**28** **Freaky Fourth Count**

R L R L L   R L R L L   R L R L L   R

*SPECIAL ASSIGNMENT: Before going to line 29, try to count and play the first measures of 25, 26, 27, and 28 straight down the page. Then do the second measures, then the third, etc. This is a great exercise in rhythm!*

**29** **All Mixed Up**

R R L R L   R L L R L   R L R R L   R

**30** **Hot Cross Buns**

R L R   R L R   R R L L R R L L R L R

**31** **Merrily We Speed Along** *Alternating sticks.*

R L R L R L R   L R L R L R   R L R L R L R   L R L R L

# LESSON 5
## The Fourth Note/Dotted Half Note Lesson

**Rudiment: Paradiddle** *Para = two consecutive alternating strokes. Diddle = two consecutive beats by the same hand. These two can be put together in any combination.*

R L R R L R L L
pa ra did dle pa ra did dle

**32** **New-Note Exercise** *Single Paradiddle.*

R L R R     L R L L     R L R R

**33** **Introducing the Dotted Half Note** *Double Paradiddle.*

R L R L R R   L R L R L L   R L R L R R   L R L R L L   R L R L R R

**34** **Low Note-High Note** *Paradiddle-diddle.*

R L R R L L   L R L L R R   R L R R L R L L   R L R R L L R

**35** **Etude for Clarinet** *Inverted Paradiddle (Diddle-para).*

R R L R L L R L R R L R L L R L R L R L R R L L R   L L R L R R L R L L R L R R L R L R L R L L R R L

**36** **Echo Song #2**

R R L L R L   R R L L R L   R R L L R   R R L L R   L L R R L   L L R R L   R L R R L   R L R R L
*solo*     *class*     *solo*     *class*     *solo*     *class*     *solo*     *all*

**37** **Go Tell Aunt Rhodie**

R R L L R L   R L L R L L   R R L L R L   R L R R L   R R L L R L   R L L R L L   R L R R L R L L   R L R

**38** **Yankee's First Half** *The entire song is in Lesson 15.*

R   L   R   R    L   R   L   L    R   R   L   L    R   L   R   L   R

**39** **Paris Duet**

R L R LL | R L R LL | R L R L | R R L   R R L | R L R LL | R L R LL | R L R L | R R L L R

**40** **Duet Part**

R R L L R R L   R R L L R R L   R L R L R   L L R   L L R R L L R R L   R R L L R R L   R L R L R R L L R

# LESSON 5
## The Fourth Note/Dotted Half Note Lesson

*A dot after a note adds one
half the value of that note.*

**32  New-Note Exercise**

**33  Introducing the Dotted Half Note**  *Write the counting on the lines below the staff.*

**34  Low Note-High Note**

**35  Etude for Clarinet**  *Watch the new sticking.*

**36  Echo Song #2**  *Paradiddle.*

**37  Go Tell Aunt Rhodie**

**38  Yankee's First Half**  *The entire song is in **Lesson 15**. Left hand lead.*

**39  Paris Duet**

**40  Duet Part**

18 *accompaniment*  19 *harmony*

# LESSON 6
## The 2/4 Lesson

**Rudiment:** **Sixteenth Notes**

**38** *sixteenth note*

R L R L R L R L
L R L R L R L R

**41** **The Most Famous Note** *Repeat many times.*
*Triple Paradiddle, or Para Para Paradiddle.*

R L R L R L R R
L R L R L R L L

**42** **Trumpet "Kick" Note** *Repeat many times.*
*Diddle In The Middle.*

R L L R L R R L

**43** **Back and Forth** *Splitting the eighth notes equals two sixteenth notes.*

R L R L R L R    R L R L R L R    R R L L R    L L R R L    R L R L R L R

**44** **Solo Line**

R L R L R L R    RL    RL    R L R L R L R    RL    RL    R L R L R L R    RL    RL    R L R L    R L R L R L R

**45** **Class Line**

R L R L R L R    RL    RL R L R L R L R    RL    RL    R L R L R L R    RL    RL    R L R L    R L R L R L R

**46** **Introducing 2/4 Time** *Watch the sticking.*

**20**

R    L    R    L    R    R    L    L    R         R    L    R    L    R    R    L    L    R

**47** **Grand Ole Duke of York**

R    R    L    L    R    L    R    R    L    L    R    L    R    L    R    R    L    L    R    L    R    L    L    R    L

**48** **Twinkle Twinkle**                                             *Ask your director why there is no double bar here!*

R L R L    R L R L R    R L R L    R L R L R    R L R L    R L R L R    R L R L    R L R L R

R L R L    R L R L R    L R L R    L R L R L    R L R L    R L R L R    L R L R    L R L R L

*SUGGESTION: Expand your warm-up to include Warm-up #2 (and play it from memory).*

# LESSON 6
## The 2/4 Lesson

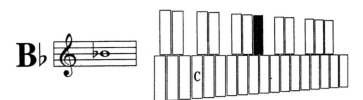  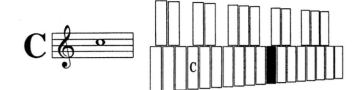

**41** **The Most Famous Note**  *Repeat many times.*

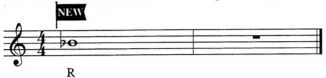

R

**42** **Trumpet "Kick" Note**  *Repeat many times.*

R

**43** **Back and Forth**

R          R          R  L  R     R  L  R     R

**44** **Solo Line**

**45** **Class Line**

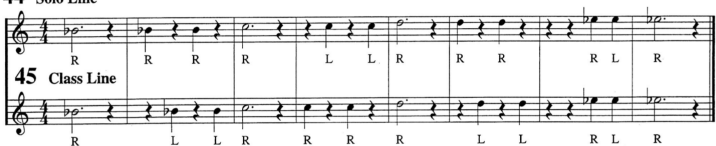

**46** **Introducing 2/4 Time**  *Watch the sticking.*

R  L   R  L   R R L L  R       R  L   R  L   R R L L  R

**47** **Grand Ole Duke of York**  *Sometimes a diddle occurs during a note change.*

R R   L L   R  L  R R L L  R   L   R L R R   L L R   L  R L L   R  L

**48** **Twinkle Twinkle**  *Ask your director why there is no double bar here!*

R R L  L  R R L   R R L L R R   L   R R L L  R R L   R R L L R R   L

R R   L L  R R L  R R   L L R R L   R R L L  R R L   R R L L R R   L

*SUGGESTION:  Expand your warm-up to include Warm-up #2 (and play it from memory).*

B-497

19

# Rhythm Set #1
### Eighth, Quarter, Half, and Whole Note Rhythms
*Use top sticking first time, bottom sticking second time.*

# Rhythm Set #1

### Eighth, Quarter, Half, and Whole Note Rhythms

*Use top sticking first time, bottom sticking second time.*

# LESSON 7
## The 3/4 Lesson

**Rudiment:** Eighth Note Buzz

**Rudiment:** Double Paradiddle

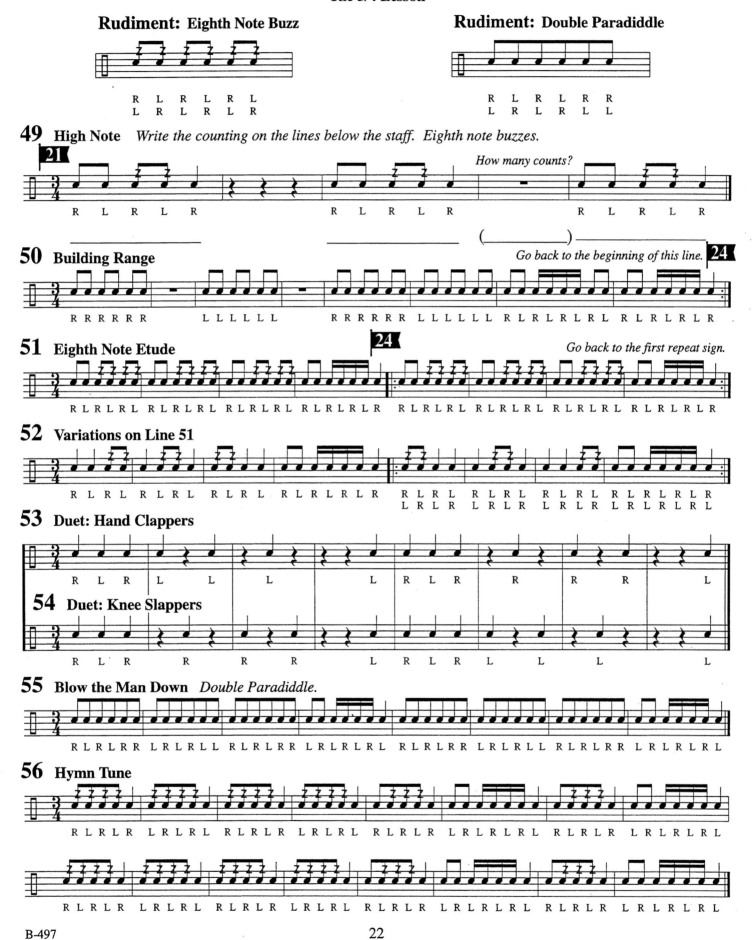

# LESSON 7
## The 3/4 Lesson

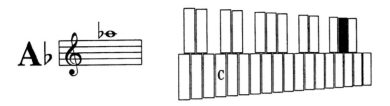

**49** **High Note** *Write the counting on the lines below the staff.*

How many counts?

R          R          R

_____     (_____)     _____
Go back to the beginning of this line.

**50** **Building Range**

R          R          R     L     R     L     R          L

**51** **Eighth Note Etude**          Go back to the first repeat sign.

R L R L R L  R   L   R     R L R L R L   R          R L R L R L   R   L   R     R L R L R L   R

**52** **Variations on Line 51**

R   L   R   L   R   L R L     R L R   L          R     L R L   R     L R L   R     L   R   L   R     L

**53** **Duet: Hand Clappers**

R   L   R     L     L          L          L          R   L   R          R          R          R          L

**54** **Duet: Knee Slappers**

R   L   R          R          R     R          L          R   L   R     L          L          L          L

**55** **Blow the Man Down**

L   R   R L     R     L L R     L   R R L     R          L   R R L     R     L     R   L L R     L

**56** **Hymn Tune**

R   L   R          L   R   L     R   L   R          L          R   L   R          L     R          L   R   L     R

R   L   R          L   R   L     R   L   R          L          R   L   R          L     L     R     L   R   L     L

# LESSON 8
## Introducing the Tie

**Rudiment: Long Buzz Roll**

# LESSON 8
## Introducing the Tie

# LESSON 9
## The Dotted Quarter Lesson

*Learn how to clean and care
for your instrument properly.*

**67** Introducing the Dotted Quarter and Eighth Rest

**68** Another Way (To Introduce the Dotted Quarter and Eighth Rest)

**69** Dotted Quarters Everywhere

**70** Song with Dotted Quarter *Alternating every tap.*

**71** America

**72** Alma Mater

**73** Careless Love

*SUGGESTION: Add the first two measures of Warm-up #3 to your daily routine.*

# LESSON 9
## The Dotted Quarter Lesson

*Learn how to clean and care*
*for your instrument properly.*

**67** **Introducing the Dotted Quarter and Eighth Rest**

*Eighth notes are sometimes written with a single flag on the stem.*

**68** **Another Way (To Introduce the Dotted Quarter and Eighth Rest)**

**69** **Dotted Quarters Everywhere**

**70** **Song with Dotted Quarter**

**71** **America**

**72** **Alma Mater**

**73** **Careless Love**

*SUGGESTION: Add the first two measures of Warm-up #3 to your daily routine.*

# Rhythm Set #2
## Dotted Quarter Rhythms

# Rhythm Set #2
## Dotted Quarter Rhythms

# LESSON 10
## Dotted Quarter Drill

**Rudiment:** **Sixteenth Note Diddles** *Make each stroke as smooth as possible.*

*You can tell how good players are by the way they look. Good players have good posture and instrument position.*

**74** **A Lower Note**

**75** **Low-Note Drill**

**76** **Dotted Quarter Drill**

**77** **Hand Clappers** *Paradiddle — diddle-para.*

**78** **Knee Slappers**

**79** **Goin' Home**

**80** **All through the Night**

**81** **Crazy Rhythm Bridge**

**82** **Duet Part**

# LESSON 10
### Dotted Quarter Drill

*You can tell how good players are by the way they look. Good players have good posture and instrument position.*

**74 A Lower Note**

**75 Low-Note Drill**

**76 Dotted Quarter Drill**

**77 Hand Clappers**

**78 Knee Slappers**

**79 Goin' Home**

**80 All through the Night**

**81 Crazy Rhythm Bridge**

**82 Duet Part**

# LESSON 11
### The Slur Lesson

**Rudiment: Flam** *The small note is a grace note and is played 0"-1" from the drum head. The big note tells you if it is a right flam or a left flam and is played 2"-8" from the drum head.*

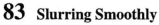

L R    r L    L R    r L

*is a right flam.*      *is a left flam.*

L R                      r L

### 83 Slurring Smoothly

L R        L R        L R  L R        L R        r L        r L        r L  r L        r L

### 84 Dedicated to Clarinets *Remember the grace note hits the drum before the big note.*

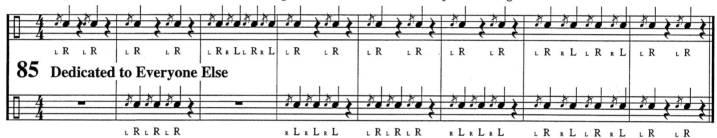

L R    L R    L R    L R    L R r L L R r L    L R    L R    L R    L R    L R    L R    L R r L L L R r L    L R    L R

### 85 Dedicated to Everyone Else

L R L R L R        r L r L r L    L R L R L R    r L r L r L    L R r L L R r L    L R    L R

### 86 High and Low Notes

L R    L R    r L r L r L    r L    r L    L R L R L R    L R    L R    r L r L r L    r L    r L    L R L R L R

### 87 French Song (with Pick-up Notes)

R L    L R    r L    L R  R L    r L R L R L    L R  L R    r L  r L    L R  L R    r L R L R L  r L

*How do you count the first two notes?*

### 88 Sweetly Sings the Donkey (Round) *Flamadiddle.*       **7** *double bar*

L R  R L  R R    r L    L R    r L R  L L    L R    r L    L R  R L  R R    r L    L R    r L R  L L    L R    r L

### 89 Aura Lee *Flam tap.*

L R L R L    L R L R  L    L R L R L    L R L  r L    r L R L R    r L R L R    r L R L R    r L R  r L

L R L  r L    r L R  r L    L R R r L L    L R r L r L    L R L R L    L R L R  L    L R L R  L    L R L R  L r L

*Congratulations! You're half-way through the book!*

# LESSON 11
## The Slur Lesson

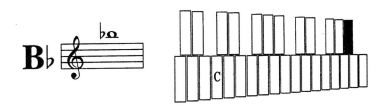

**83** **Slurring Smoothly**

**84** **Dedicated to Clarinets**

NEW

**85** **Dedicated to Everyone Else**

**86** **High and Low Notes**

**87** **French Song (with Pick-up Notes)**

*How do you count the first two notes?*

**88** **Sweetly Sings the Donkey (Round)**

double bar

pa ra did dle

**89** **Aura Lee**

*Congratulations! You're half-way through the book!*

# LESSON 12
### Building the Chalameau

# LESSON 12
## Building the Chalameau

# Supplementary Lesson

### For Snare Drum Only

**A** *All the following sixteenth notes utilize "standard sticking" – all down and up beats are played with the right hand, all other beats with the left hand.*

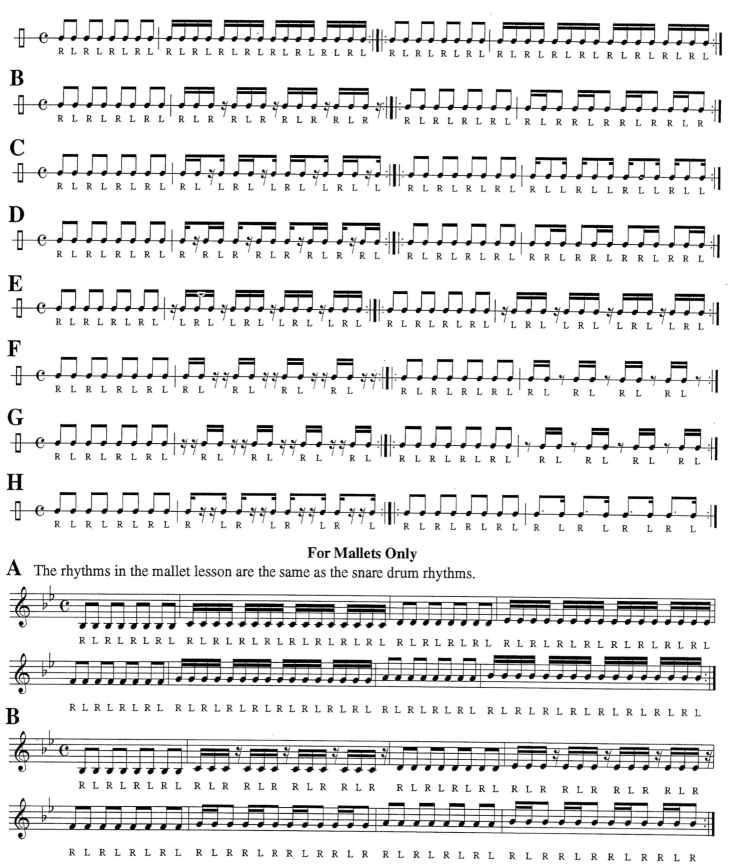

### For Mallets Only

**A** The rhythms in the mallet lesson are the same as the snare drum rhythms.

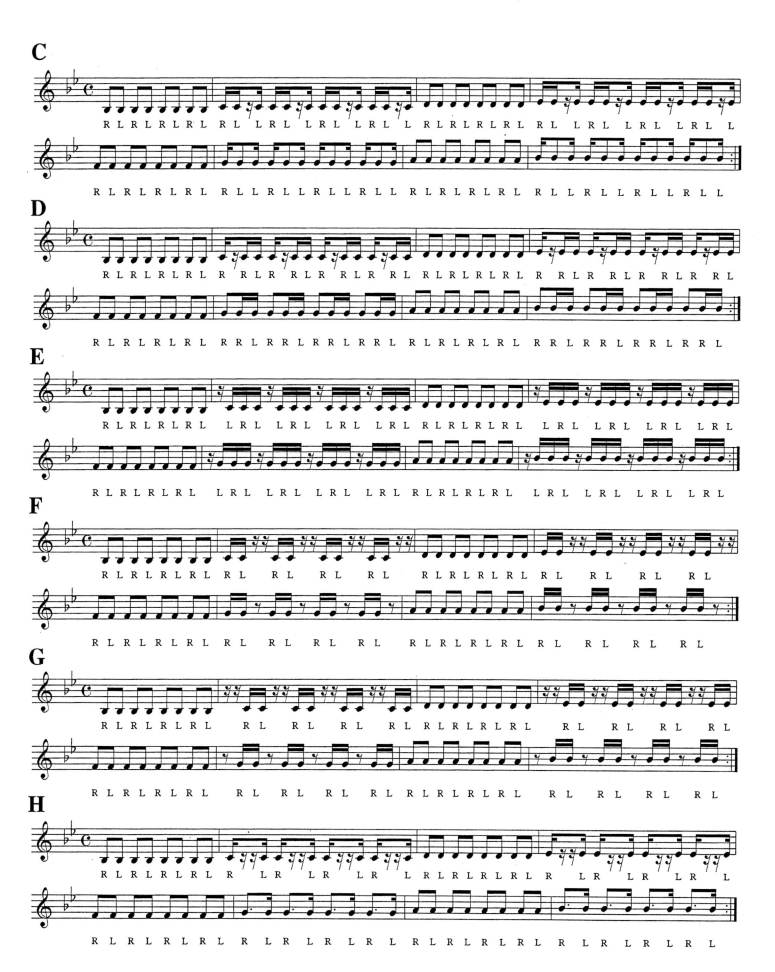

# LESSON 13

**Rudiment: Open Roll**

**Clarinet High Register**

**Rudiment: Thirty-second Note Diddle**

RRLLRRLLRRLLRRLL

**98 "The" Scale**

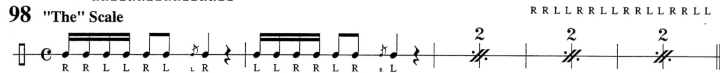

**99 Clarinets' Line**

**100 Clarinets Higher** *Adding a slash doubles, or "diddles," the note marked.*

**101 Clarinets Higher Still** *Traditionally, rolls are marked with 3 slashes. This exercise sounds the same as 100.*

**102 Barcarolle** *Accented paradiddle patterns.*

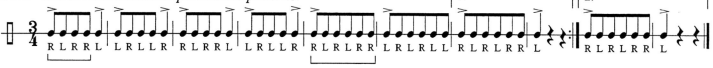

**103 Barcarolle Again** *Dedicated to clarinets. First time, play the sixteenth notes without the diddles (rolls).*

**104 One More Song**

*SUGGESTION: Gradually add all of Warm-up #3 to your daily routine.*

# LESSON 13
## Clarinet High Register

**98** "The" Scale *Octaves (double stops) mean to play two notes at the same time.*

**99** Clarinets' Line

**100** Clarinets Higher

**101** Clarinets Higher Still

**102** Barcarolle

**103** Barcarolle Again *Dedicated to clarinets.*

**104** One More Song

*SUGGESTION: Gradually add all of Warm-up #3 to your daily routine.*

# LESSON 14
**Introducing Dynamics**

Dynamics/Stick Height (see Introductory Lesson)

| | | | |
|---|---|---|---|
| *pp* | 0" - 1.5" | *p* | 1.5" - 3" |
| *mp* | 3" - 4.5" | *mf* | 4.5" - 6" |
| *f* | 6" - 7.5" | *ff* | 7.5" - 9" |

**105** Loud Etude

**106** Soft Exercise *Does this sound familiar?*

**107** Swing Low

**108** Mexican Song

**109** Duet: Part One

**110** Duet: Part Two

**111** Clarinets Can't Play This Now - Maybe Later?

# LESSON 14
## Introducing Dynamics

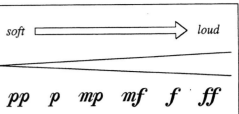

*There is no sticking on this lesson. See
if you can figure it out on your own!*

**105  Loud Etude**

**32**  *f*

**106  Soft Exercise**  *Does this sound familiar?*

*p*

**107  Swing Low**

*p*    *mp*    *mf* ——————— *f*

*f*    *mf*    *mp* ——————— *pp*

**108  Mexican Song**

*p*    *f*    *p*    *f*

**109  Duet: Part One**

*f*    *p*    *f*    *ff*

**110  Duet: Part Two**

*p*    *f*    *p*    *ff*

**111  Clarinets Can't Play This Now - Maybe Later?**

*f*

# LESSON 15
## The Key Signature Lesson

*See page 62 for the Five-stroke roll and the Nine-stroke roll.*

**112** **Yankee Doodle with Key Signature**

**113** **Same Song, Different Key**

**114** **Mary Ann**

**115** **Etude in Three Keys**

# LESSON 15
## The Key Signature Lesson

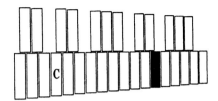 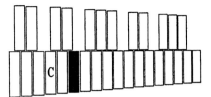

*A note "out of key" is a wrong note.*

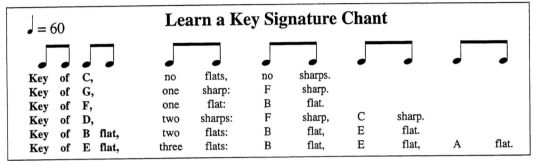

**Learn a Key Signature Chant**

♩ = 60

| Key of C, | no flats, | no sharps. |
| Key of G, | one sharp: | F sharp. |
| Key of F, | one flat: | B flat. |
| Key of D, | two sharps: | F sharp, C sharp. |
| Key of B flat, | two flats: | B flat, E flat. |
| Key of E flat, | three flats: | B flat, E flat, A flat. |

*Later, your director will perhaps give you a specific chant for each line.*

**112  Yankee Doodle with Key Signature**

**113  Same Song, Different Key**

**114  Mary Ann**

**115  Etude in Three Keys**

*Key of B flat, two flats: B flat, E flat.*

*Key of F, one flat: B flat.*

*Key of E flat, three flats: B flat, E flat, A flat.*

# LESSON 16
## The Cut-Time Lesson

*A great deal of music is written in cut-time. Composers like it because it is less work to write.*

**116** Scale in Cut-Time

**117** Cut-Time Compared

**118** Same Line, Different Time

**119** Good King Wenceslas

**120** Michael, Row the Boat Ashore

**121** Lightly Row *Remember the buzz?*

**122** Marine's Hymn

# LESSON 16
### The Cut-Time Lesson

*A great deal of music is written in cut-time. Composers like it because it is less work to write.*

**116** Scale in Cut-Time

**117** Cut-Time Compared

**118** Same Line, Different Time

**119** Good King Wenceslas

**120** Michael, Row the Boat Ashore

**121** Lightly Row

**122** Marine's Hymn

*All successful players are rhythmically independent.*

*You must be able to play your part while others perform different music.*

**123** Variations on "Sol-La-Ti-Do"

**124** Oom-Pa

**125** Duet Part

**126** John Jacob Jingle

*All successful players are rhythmically independent.*

*You must be able to play your part while others perform different music.*

**123** **Variations on "Sol-La-Ti-Do"**

**124** **Oom-Pa**

**125** **Duet Part**

**126** **John Jacob Jingle** *Double stops: play two notes at the same time.*

# LESSON 18
## Syncopation

*Always play up-beat notes exactly on the up-beat, not early.*

**127** Syncopation  **37**

**128** Syncopation Exercise

**129** Our Boys Will Shine (Shortened Version)

**130** Camptown Races  *Where are the syncopated notes?*

**131** Mixed-Up McDonald

**132** Tom Dooley

**133** Accompaniment

# LESSON 18
### Syncopation

*Always play up-beat notes exactly on the up-beat, not early.*

# LESSON 19
### Building Rhythmic Independence

# LESSON 19
### Building Rhythmic Independence

**134** **Counting Syncopation**

**135** **Syncopation in Cut-Time**

**136** **Good Night, Ladies**

**137** **Dem Bones**

**138** **March for Hand-Clappers, Knee-Slappers, Finger-Snappers, and Foot-Stompers**

# Optional Supplementary Rhythm Set
## Sixteenth Notes

### 3/8 and 6/8 (Compound) Time

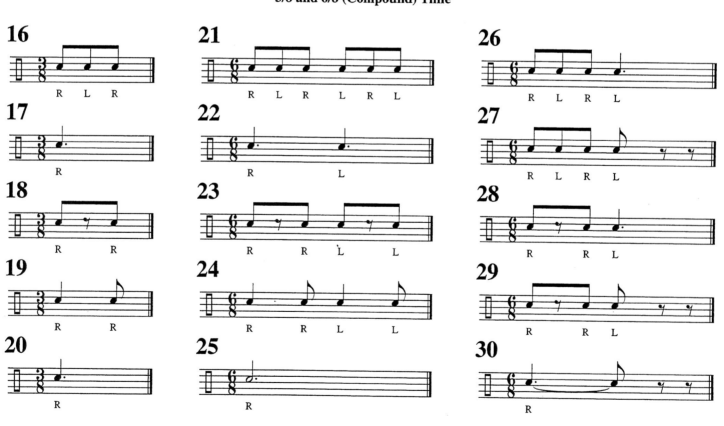

# Optional Supplementary Rhythm Set
## Sixteenth Notes

# Optional Supplementary Lesson #1
## Sixteenth Notes

*See page 62 for the Seven-stroke roll.*

**A  Scale with Sixteenth Notes**

**B  Bird**

**C  Polly Wolly Doodle**

**D  Ring-a-Ding-a-Ding**

**E  Scale with Two Sixteenths**

**F  Skip to My Lou**

# Optional Supplementary Lesson #1
### Sixteenth Notes

*Try to figure out where to
play any unfamiliar notes
you may find on this page.*

**A** Scale with Sixteenth Notes

**B** Bird

**C** Polly Wolly Doodle

**D** Ring-a-Ding-a-Ding

**E** Scale with Two Sixteenths

**F** Skip to My Lou

# Optional Supplementary Lesson #2
## 6/8 and 3/8 Time

*See page 63 for the Flam Accent and the Flam Tap.*

# Optional Supplementary Lesson #2
## 6/8 and 3/8 Time

**A**  6/8 Scale

**B**  Piano Duet

**C**  Duet Part

**D**  Farmer Song

*Watch out!*

**E**  Southern Roses Waltz in 3/8 Time

**F**  Hymn Song

**G**  Lovely Evening Round

B-497

57

*Percussion Only*

# Special Songs for Individual Practice

**Up on the Housetop**

**America**

**Red River Valley**

**Skip To My Lou**

**Reveille**

# Special Songs for Individual Practice

*Try to figure out where to play any unfamiliar notes you may find on this page.*

**Up on the Housetop**

**America**

**Red River Valley**

**Skip To My Lou**

**Reveille**

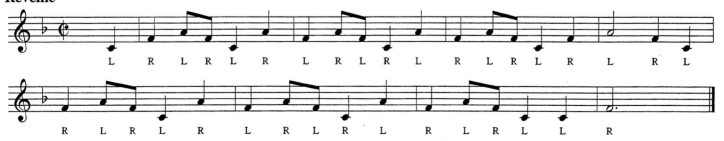

# Special Songs for Individual Practice

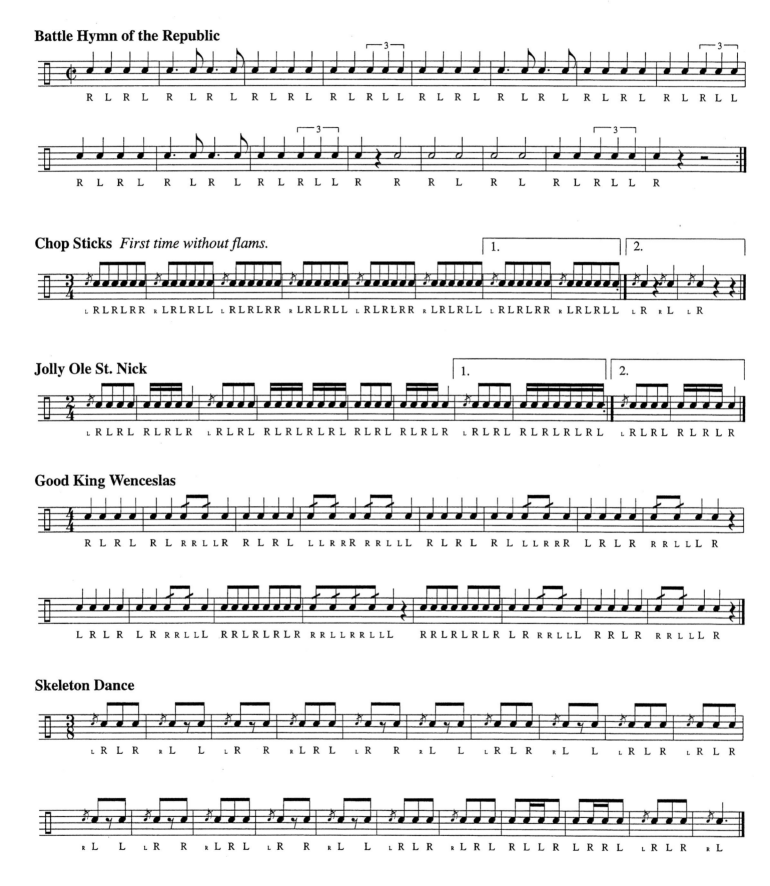

**Battle Hymn of the Republic**

**Chop Sticks** *First time without flams.*

**Jolly Ole St. Nick**

**Good King Wenceslas**

**Skeleton Dance**

# Special Songs for Individual Practice

*Try to figure out where to play any unfamiliar notes you may find on this page.*

**Battle Hymn of the Republic**

**Chop Sticks** *Stems up played with the right hand, stems down with the left.*

**Jolly Ole St. Nick**

**Good King Wenceslas**

**Skeleton Dance**

# Scales to Prepare for Book Two

**F Concert Major Scale**

**E Flat Concert Major Scale**

**B Flat Concert Major Scale**

**B Flat Concert Chromatic Scale**

B-497

61

# Percussive Arts Society
# International Drum Rudiments

*All rudiments should be practiced: open (slow) to close (fast) and/or at an even moderate march tempo.*

## I. Roll Rudiments

### A. Single Stroke Roll Rudiments

1. *Single Stroke Roll\**

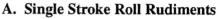

R L R L R L R L

2. *Single Stroke Four*

R L R L    R L R L
L R L R    L R L R

3. *Single Stroke Seven*

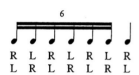

R L R L R L R
L R L R L R L

### B. Multiple Bounce Roll Rudiments

4. *Multiple Bounce Roll*

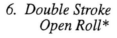

R R R R r L L L L l

5. *Triple Stroke Roll*

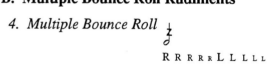

R R R L L L R R R L L L

### C. Double Stroke Open Roll Rudiments

6. *Double Stroke Open Roll\**

R R L L R R L L

7. *Five Stroke Roll\**

R    R    L    L

8. *Six Stroke Roll*

R    L    R    L
L    R    L    R

9. *Seven Stroke Roll\**

R    L    R    L
L    R    L    R

10. *Nine Stroke Roll\**

R    R    L    L

11. *Ten Stroke Roll\**

R R L    R R L
L L R    L L R

12. *Eleven Stroke Roll\**

R R L    R R L
L L R    L L R

13. *Thirteen Stroke Roll\**

R    R    L    L

14. *Fifteen Stroke Roll\**

R    L R    L
L    R L    R

15. *Seventeen Stroke Roll*

R    R    L    L

## II. Diddle Rudiments

16. *Single Paradiddle\**

R L R R L R L L

17. *Double Paradiddle\**

R L R L R R L R L R L L

18. *Triple Paradiddle*

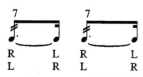

R L R L R L R R L R L R L R L L

19. *Single Paradiddle-diddle*

R L R R L L R L R R L L
L R L L R R L R L L R R

*\*These rudiments are also included in the original Standard 26 American Drum Rudiments.*

# III. Flam Rudiments

### IV. Drag Rudiments

20. *Flam**

31. *Drag**

21. *Flam Accent**

32. *Single Drag Tap**

22. *Flam Tap**

33. *Double Drag Tap**

23. *Flamacue*

34. *Lesson 25**

24. *Flam Paradiddle**

35. *Single Dragadiddle*

25. *Single Flammed Mill*

36. *Drag Paradiddle #1**

26. *Flam Paradiddle-diddle**

37. *Drag Paradiddle #2**

27. *Pataflafla*

38. *Single Ratamacue**

28. *Swiss Army Triplet*

39. *Double Ratamacue**

29. *Inverted Flam Tap*

40. *Triple Ratamacue**

30. *Flam Drag*

B-497

# Traditional "One And" Counting System*

Most teachers of band instruments agree that the teaching of music reading can be done most efficiently and effectively with a counting system. A rhythmic vocabulary helps communication and promotes understanding. It doesn't seem to matter which counting system is used as long as there is a system and it is used consistently. Two suggested counting systems are offered on these two pages.

The idea of saying the "number" of the count on which a note occurs and saying the word, "and," for any note that occurs half-way after the beat has been used for many years. The basic idea with many variations can be found in hundreds of music books. Probably the most widely circulated publication using this system of counting is the *Haskell Harr Drum Method*. Because of its long history (published in 1937 and still used today), its expansive use, and the general public perception that percussionists are supposedly experts at counting, many band directors have adapted a counting system that is remarkably similar. The following is a somewhat modified summary of "one and" counting that might be used by teachers and students for this band method:

---

### I. Notes of One or More Counts

For notes of one count (or longer), simply say the number of the count on which the note begins and continue counting for the duration of the note. Thus, a note which receives one count and which begins on the first beat of the measure would be counted, "one." If the note occurs on the second count say, "two," etc. A note of longer value would simply be counted longer. The following example quickly illustrates the counting system as applied to rhythms (including rests) of one, two, three, or four counts:

### II. Counting the Sub-divisions

Notes which receive less than a whole count and which are divisible by two (some would say simple time) are counted as follows:

Notes which receive less than a whole count and which are divisible by three (some would say compound time) are counted as follows:

---

*For a complete explanation of this counting system, see *the Haskell Harr Drum Method*, published by M. M. Cole Publishing Company.

# Eastman Counting System*

there is no "official" counting system endorsed by the Eastman School of Music, there was a system written by Alan I. McHose which was published in his series of theory texts. Because he was a theory instructor at the Eastman School for many years and his books were used as textbooks for his theory classes, most Eastman students of the 1940s, 50s, and 60s used his counting syllables.

For almost a third of a century these graduates of one of America's largest and most highly regarded music schools have been doing a great deal of "evangelizing" about their counting system. Many have been leaders in music education and their teaching techniques have been widely copied. The authors of this band method, neither of whom attended the Eastman School, have adapted the system and used a modified version in teaching beginning band classes. Both recommend its use with this band method.

## I. Notes of One or More Counts

Notes of one count (or longer) are counted much the same way as in any other counting system. One major difference is that notes longer than one count are held with a continuous word-sound. Thus, a whole note in 4/4 time would be counted, "onnnnnnnnne," for four counts. The following example quickly illustrates the counting system as applied to rhythms (including rests) of one, two, three, or four counts:

## II. Counting the Sub-divisions

Notes which receive less than a whole count are categorized into rhythms which are divisible by two or those which are divisible by three (some would say duple and triple rhythms). Again, any note which occurs on a downbeat is simply counted with the number of the count. The important difference is that a note which occurs on the last half of a count is counted, "te," (Latin, rhymes with May) and notes which occur on the second or third fraction of the count are counted; "lah," and, "lee." Everything else is counted, "ta" (pronounced, "tah").

Rhythms Which are Divisible by Two (Read Down)     Rhythms Which are Divisible by Three (Read Down)

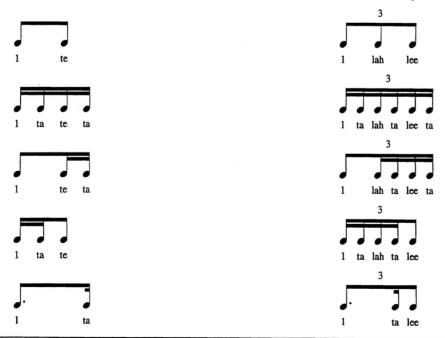

*For a complete explanation of this counting system, see the *Ear Training and Sight Singing Dictation Manual*, published by Prentice Hall.

65

# Warm-ups

*Play a good, strong tone.*

# Practice Record Chart

| Week | Day 1 | Day 2 | Day 3 | Day 4 | Day 5 | Day 6 | Day 7 | Total Time | Parent's Initials | Weekly Grade | Week | Day 1 | Day 2 | Day 3 | Day 4 | Day 5 | Day 6 | Day 7 | Total Time | Parent's Initials | Weekly Grade |
|---|---|---|---|---|---|---|---|---|---|---|---|---|---|---|---|---|---|---|---|---|---|
| 1 | | | | | | | | | | | 19 | | | | | | | | | | |
| 2 | | | | | | | | | | | 20 | | | | | | | | | | |
| 3 | | | | | | | | | | | 21 | | | | | | | | | | |
| 4 | | | | | | | | | | | 22 | | | | | | | | | | |
| 5 | | | | | | | | | | | 23 | | | | | | | | | | |
| 6 | | | | | | | | | | | 24 | | | | | | | | | | |
| 7 | | | | | | | | | | | 25 | | | | | | | | | | |
| 8 | | | | | | | | | | | 26 | | | | | | | | | | |
| 9 | | | | | | | | | | | 27 | | | | | | | | | | |
| 10 | | | | | | | | | | | 28 | | | | | | | | | | |
| 11 | | | | | | | | | | | 29 | | | | | | | | | | |
| 12 | | | | | | | | | | | 30 | | | | | | | | | | |
| 13 | | | | | | | | | | | 31 | | | | | | | | | | |
| 14 | | | | | | | | | | | 32 | | | | | | | | | | |
| 15 | | | | | | | | | | | 33 | | | | | | | | | | |
| 16 | | | | | | | | | | | 34 | | | | | | | | | | |
| 17 | | | | | | | | | | | 35 | | | | | | | | | | |
| 18 | | | | | | | | | | | 36 | | | | | | | | | | |

# Index of Musical Terms

**1** **Staff** - the five lines and four spaces where notes are placed

**2** **Treble Clef** - a symbol that indicates which notes are on each line and space of the staff; also called the "G" clef

**3** **Bass Clef** - a symbol that indicates which notes are on each line and space of the staff; also called the "F" clef

**4** **Bar Line** - divides the staff into measures

**5** **Measure** - the space between two bar lines

**6** **4/4 Time Signature** - The numeral on top indicates that there are four beats in each measure. The bottom numeral indicates that each quarter note gets one beat.

**7** **Double Bar** - marks the end of a section

**8** **Whole Note** - gets four beats in any time signature with a 4 as the bottom numeral, such as 4/4 time; equivalent to two half notes

**9** **Whole Rest** - gets four beats in any time signature with a 4 as the bottom numeral (except 3/4); equivalent to two half rests

**10** **Quarter Note** - gets one beat in any time signature with a 4 as the bottom numeral; equivalent to two eighth notes

**11** **Quarter Rest** - gets one beat in any time signature with a 4 as the bottom numeral; equivalent to two eighth rests

**12** **Half Note** - gets two beats in any time signature with a 4 as the bottom numeral; equivalent to two quarter notes

**13** **Half Rest** - gets two beats in any time signature with a 4 as the bottom numeral; equivalent to two quarter rests

**14** **Duet** - a song for two players or two parts

**15** **Solo** - means that the part is to be played by one person

**16** **Eighth Note** - gets half a beat in any time signature with a 4 as the bottom numeral; equivalent to two sixteenth notes

**17** **Dotted Half Note** - gets three beats in any time signature with a 4 as the bottom numeral; equivalent to three quarter notes

**18** **Accompaniment** - a part that supports the melody but is subordinate to it

**19** **Harmony** - the consonant sounding of two or more notes together

**20** **2/4 Time Signature** - two beats in each measure; each quarter note gets one beat.

**21** **3/4 Time Signature** - three beats in each measure; each quarter note gets one beat.

**22** **Eighth Rest** - gets half a beat in any time signature with a 4 as the bottom numeral

**23** **Afterbeat** - a note played on the second half of the beat

**24** **Repeat Sign** - means to go back to the beginning of the song or section

**25** **Tie** - combines the durations of two notes of the same pitch

**26** **First and Second Endings** - play through the first ending, repeat, then skip the first ending and play through the second ending

**27** **Round** - music for two or more in which the performers play the same music but start and end at different times

**28** **Dotted Quarter Note** - gets one and one half beats in any time signature with a 4 as the bottom numeral; equivalent to three eighth notes

**29** **Slur** - a line connecting two or more notes which indicates that only the first note joined by the slur is to be tongued

**30** **Pick-up Note/Notes** - the notes in an incomplete measure at the beginning of a song; note values are usually taken from the last measure

**31** **Common Time Signature** - the same as 4/4 time

**32** **Dynamics** - indicate the relative volume of a note or notes

**33** **Key Signature** - sharps or flats placed at the beginning of a section indicating that certain notes are to be sharped or flatted throughout that section

**34** **Cut-time** - the same as 2/2 time; two beats in each measure; each half note gets one beat.

**35** **Fine** - marks the end of the song

**36** **D.C. al Fine** - means to go back to the beginning of the song and play until "Fine" is reached

**37** **Syncopation** - an accented note (or stressed note) that comes on an unaccented beat; frequently a note that starts on the up-beat and is held through the next downbeat

**38** **Sixteenth Note** - gets one fourth of a beat in any time signature with a 4 as the bottom numeral

**39** **6/8 Time Signature** - two beats in each measure; each dotted quarter note gets one beat.

**40** **3/8 Time Signature** - one beat in each measure; each dotted quarter note gets one beat.

**41** **Fermata** - means to hold the note longer than the indicated value

**42** **Flat** - lowers a note one half step

**43** **Sharp** - raises a note one half step

**44** **Natural** - cancels the effect of a sharp or flat

**45** **Repeat Measure** - means to repeat the preceding measure

**46** **Double Repeat Measure** - means to repeat the preceding two measures

# Selected Snare Drum Publications

## COLLECTIONS

### MARONI, JOE

**B565**    **Fifty Elementary Duets for Snare Drum**    HL3770910

"50 Elementary Duets for Snare Drum" is designed to help fill the gap between the elementary and intermediate levels of snare drum playing.  These duets are presented in several different time signatures with suggested metronome markings, each one utilizing a different rhythmic theme.  Benefits for playing the material in this book include: 1. Opportunity to play along with another person, 2. Opportunity to play with a metronome, 2. Develop an ability to read different time signatures, and 4. Acquire a repertoire of snare drum literature.

### SCHINSTINE, WILLIAM J

**B169SP**    **Little Champ First Year Drum Solos**    HL3770251
Percussion Music

## SOLO, UNACCOMPANIED

### GOMEZ/ RIFE

**B463**    **International Style Etudes, Vol. 2 (Grade 2)**    HL3770681

This second of two volumes is a collection of timpani etudes for educational study or recital performance.  The book is divided into four categories: Latin, American, Eastern, and South American.  Each category presents stylistic concepts form the represented culture.

### SCHINSTINE, WILLIAM J

**SS612**    **Doodlers Delight (Grade 2)**    HL3774255

This piece is a fine selection for the beginning to intermediate player to use at contest or recital.  It focuses on rudiments including: flams, rolls, and paradiddles.

**B249**    **Tymp Tunes (Grade 2)**    HL3770349

This collection includes solos which are on contest lists throughout the world.  It also contains six works written specifically for this collection.  A variey of difficulty levels and music of differing styles are included, and it incorporates many technical issues found in modern tympani repertoire.  Movement titles for 2 Drums: 1. Pauken Parade, 2. The Copper Bowls, 3. Kettle Kaper, 4. Tall Tale for Tympani, 5. Tympanic, 6. Swingsation, 7. Jazz a Little Waltz, 8. Tympani Bossa Nova, 9. Academic Episode, 10. Topical Tymps.  Movement titles for 3 Drums: 1. Tymptation, 2. A Scary Scherzo, 3. Experience in Six, 4. Dresen Dance.  Movement titles for 4 Drums: 1. Slightly Latin, 2. Cake Walk for Kettles, 3. Fanfare for Four Tympani.  Snare Drum and Tympani Duet title: Dubious Debate.  Multiple Percussion Solo title: The Tympercussionist

### UKENA, TODD

**ST584**    **Accent Fever (Grade 2)**    HL3775321

As the title suggests, accents as well as dynamics are the emphasis in this short contest solo for two pitched drums (snares, tomtoms or rototoms).

**ST747**    **Devil, Daniel and Duane, The (Grade 2)**    HL3775550

A single movement gigue for mallet instrument and piano, with a middle section in Bb major with D minor at the begginning and end.  Todd A. Ukena is a composer and arranger of percussion literature and has been playing percussion since 1970.

## SOLO WITH PIANO

### SCHINSTINE, WILLIAM J
*Rose, Charles*

**SS413**    **Tympendium**    HL3774061

## TRIO

### BELLSON, LOUIE

**ST570**    **Tea for Three (Grade 2)**    HL3775306
A snare drum trio well suited for beginning level players.

### MARONI, JOE

**SU312**    **Three to Go (Grade 2)**    HL3776201

### PRENTICE, HAROLD F.

**SS103**    **Chinese Laundry Man (Grade 2)**    HL3773703

## QUARTET

### LEFEVER, MAXINE

**ST491**    **And Four to Go (Grade 2)**    HL3775201

This short quartet for unpitched percussion includes the following instruments: tom-tom (1-3 players), snare drum (1-3 players), bass drum, and suspended cymbal.

### SCHINSTINE, WILLIAM J

**SS149**    **Rhythm Busters (Grade 2)**    HL3773753

### SPEARS, JARED

**ST119**    **Prologue and Fight (Grade 2)**    HL3774706

## QUINTET

### LEFEVER, MAXINE

**ST495**    **Quint Capers (Grade 2)**    HL3775205

### SCHINSTINE, WILLIAM J

**SS911**    **Centralization (Grade 2)**    HL3774596

### TRADITIONAL
*Weinberg, Norman*

**ST702**    **Bells Of Dunkirk (Grade 2)**    HL3775489
This lively Scottish folk-tune setting features solo sections for each player.

## SEXTET

### SCHINSTINE, WILLIAM J

**ST413**    **Young Lions, The (Grade 2)**    HL3775094

This percussion sextet can be expanded by using as many keyboard percussion players as are available.  The "Young Lions" was first performed in Pottstown, PA in June 1982.